Musical Instruments

Flute

By Nick Rebman

www.littlebluehousebooks.com

Little Blue House is distributed by North Star Editions:
sales@northstareditions.com | 888-417-0195

Produced for Little Blue House by Red Line Editorial.

Photographs ©: Shutterstock Images, cover, 4, 7, 8–9, 11, 12–13, 15, 16–17, 19, 20–21, 22–23, 24 (top left), 24 (top right), 24 (bottom left), 24 (bottom right)

Library of Congress Control Number: 2022910651

ISBN
978-1-64619-699-9 (hardcover)
978-1-64619-731-6 (paperback)
978-1-64619-792-7 (ebook pdf)
978-1-64619-763-7 (hosted ebook)

Printed in the United States of America
Mankato, MN
012023

About the Author

Nick Rebman is a writer and editor who lives in Minnesota. He enjoys reading, walking his dog, and playing rock songs on his drum set.

Table of Contents

I Play the Flute

I have a flute.

I like to make music.

I blow over the hole.

Air goes through my flute.

It makes a high sound.

I press the keys.

They make the sound higher or lower.

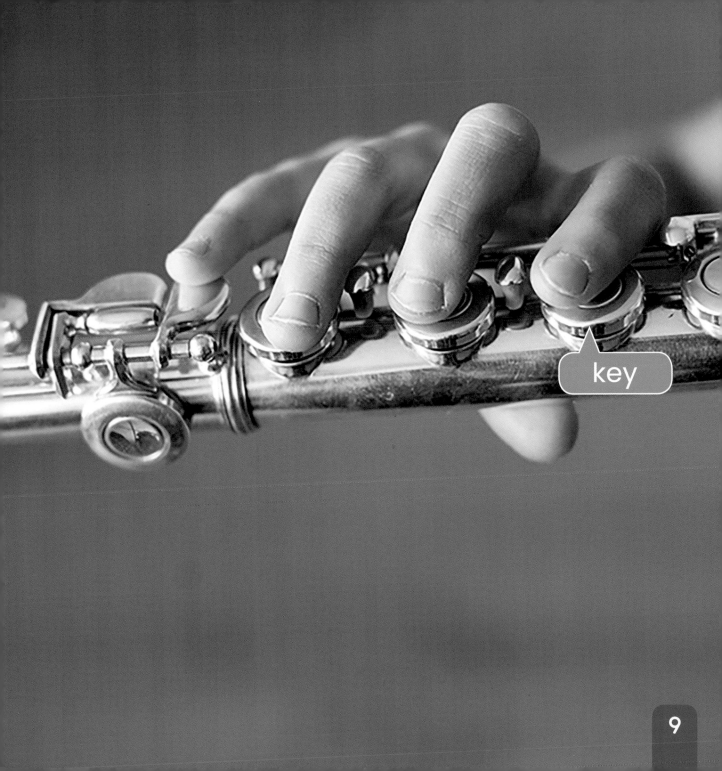

I have a teacher.

She helps me learn how to play.

11

I learn how to read sheet music.

I can play a song.

sheet music

I play the song many times.
I get better every day.

My friend can read music too.

We play a song together.

I play my flute at school.

I practice by myself.

I play my flute at home.

My cat likes to listen.

I play my flute
with friends.
We play in a band.

band

Glossary

hole

sheet music

keys

teacher

Index